branch

leaves

twig

outer bark

inner bark

trunk

roots

Be a Friend to
Trees

Be a Friend to Trees

BY Patricia Lauber

ILLUSTRATED BY Holly Keller

HarperCollins*Publishers*

The *Let's-Read-and-Find-Out Science* book series was originated by Dr. Franklyn M. Branley, Astronomer Emeritus and former Chairman of the American Museum–Hayden Planetarium, and was formerly co-edited by him and Dr. Roma Gans, Professor Emeritus of Childhood Education, Teachers College, Columbia University. Text and illustrations for each of the books in the series are checked for accuracy by an expert in the relevant field. For a complete catalog of Let's-Read-and-Find-Out Science books, write to HarperCollins Children's Books, 10 East 53rd Street, New York, NY 10022.

HarperCollins®, 🏠®, and Let's Read-and-Find-Out Science®
are trademarks of HarperCollins Publishers Inc.

BE A FRIEND TO TREES

10 ❖

Library of Congress Cataloging-in-Publication Data
Lauber, Patricia.
   Be a friend to trees / by Patricia Lauber ; illustrated by Holly Keller.
      p.   cm. — (Let's-read-and-find-out science. Stage 2)
   Summary: Discusses the importance of trees as sources of food, oxygen, and other essential things.
   ISBN 0-06-021528-3 — ISBN 0-06-021529-1 (lib. bdg.) — 0-06-445120-8 (pbk.)
   1. Trees—Juvenile literature.   2. Trees—Utilization—Juvenile literature.   [1. Trees.]   I. Keller, Holly, ill.   II. Title.   III. Series.
QK475.8.L38   1994   92-24082
582.16—dc20   CIP
                                                                                  AC

Trees are nice. They're nice to look at, nice to have around.

5

Shagbark
Hickory

Sugar Maple

6

Eastern White Pine

Gray Birch

Trees are also useful.

Both people and animals need trees of all kinds, sizes,
and shapes.

7

Everything that is made of wood was once part of a tree. Look around you. How many wooden things do you see? Make a list—don't forget to count your pencil and maybe your house.

White Oak

GRANT ORCHARD

9

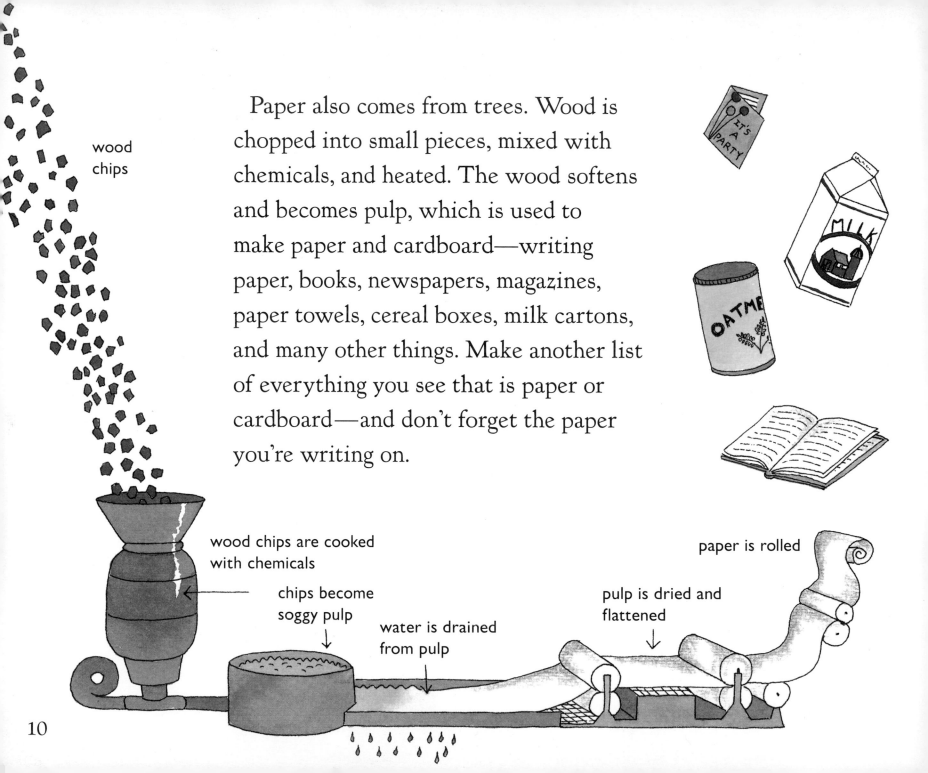

wood chips

Paper also comes from trees. Wood is chopped into small pieces, mixed with chemicals, and heated. The wood softens and becomes pulp, which is used to make paper and cardboard—writing paper, books, newspapers, magazines, paper towels, cereal boxes, milk cartons, and many other things. Make another list of everything you see that is paper or cardboard—and don't forget the paper you're writing on.

wood chips are cooked with chemicals

chips become soggy pulp

water is drained from pulp

pulp is dried and flattened

paper is rolled

10

Sugar Maple

White Pine

Rubber Tree

gums for turpentine

sap for syrup

latex for rubber

Some trees can be tapped for their sap. Sap from different trees is used to make maple syrup, chewing gum, soap, paint thinner, and rubber.

Trees are green plants, and so they make their own food. Green plants are the only living things that can do this. Other living things depend on green plants for food. Some eat parts of plants. Some eat the plant eaters. Some eat both.

You eat the parts of trees known as fruits and nuts—apples, oranges, pears, cherries, peaches, walnuts, almonds, pecans, hazelnuts, and lots of others.

Chocolate also comes from a tree. It is made from the seeds of cacao trees.

Common Walnut

Valencia Orange

Rome Apples

Queen Ann Cherries

Many animals eat parts of trees.
Caterpillars eat leaves.

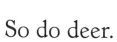

Live Oak

White Ash

So do deer.

So do koalas.

Eucalyptus

14

Acacia

And so do giraffes and elephants.

Porcupines eat the inner bark of trees, as well as buds and twigs.

Mulberry

Northern Red
Oak

16

Scarlet Hawthorn (fruit)

Squirrels and chipmunks gather nuts to eat.

Bees find food in the flowers of trees. They collect pollen and the sugary liquid called nectar.

Birds eat seeds and fruits from trees.

And those are only a few of the animals that find their food in trees.

Scarlet Hawthorn (flower)

Many animals make their homes in trees.

Birds roost in trees. They build nests and raise their young in trees.

Squirrels nest in trees.

Monkeys live in trees.

Some tree frogs spend their whole lives
in trees, without ever coming down.

19

Honeybees make hives in tree hollows.

Many other insects also live in trees.
So do small creatures such as spiders.

Deer find shelter beneath the trees of forests
and woodlands. They find safe places to hide
their young.

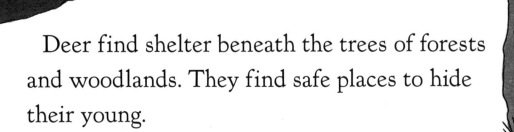

The roots of trees hold soil in place. They keep it from washing away in heavy rains or floods of water from melting snow. When soil is held in place, water sinks into it and is stored in the ground. Many people depend on water that is stored underground. They draw it to the surface through wells.

rain

groundwater

Trees do something else that is very important. It has to do with the air we breathe.

Air is made of gases. One of them is oxygen. It is the gas that our bodies need. It is the gas that all animals need.

Each time we breathe, we take oxygen out of the air. But the supply is never used up. The reason is that trees and other green plants keep putting oxygen into the air. They give off oxygen as they make their food.

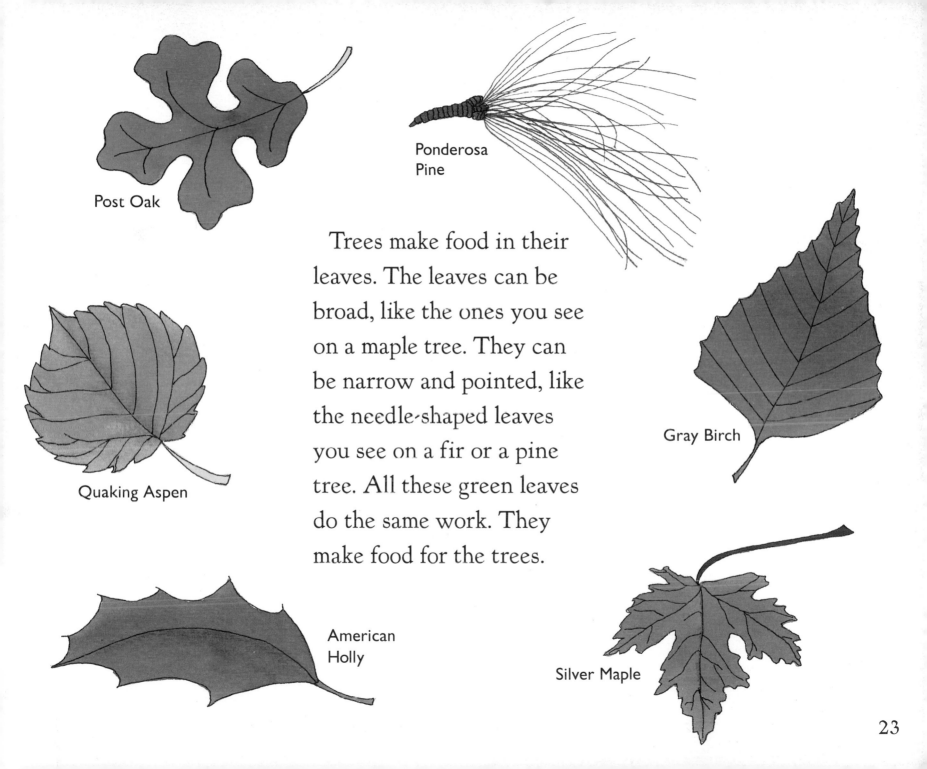

Post Oak

Ponderosa Pine

Quaking Aspen

Gray Birch

American Holly

Silver Maple

Trees make food in their leaves. The leaves can be broad, like the ones you see on a maple tree. They can be narrow and pointed, like the needle-shaped leaves you see on a fir or a pine tree. All these green leaves do the same work. They make food for the trees.

To make food, leaves use water, which they take from the ground.

They use a gas called carbon dioxide, which they take from the air.

They use sunlight as energy.

With energy from the sun, green leaves put the water and carbon dioxide together. They make a kind of sugar. The making of food by plants is called photosynthesis, a word that means "putting together with light."

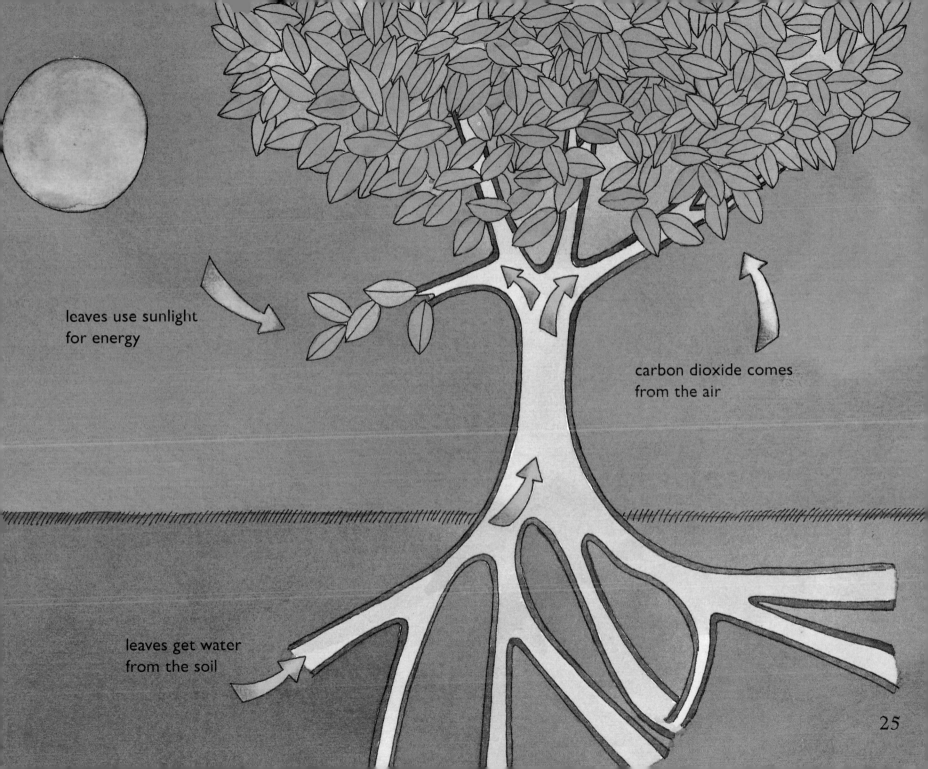

leaves use sunlight
for energy

carbon dioxide comes
from the air

leaves get water
from the soil

25

twig with new buds for leaves and flowers

Red Mulberry

Trees need food just to stay alive. They also need food for growth—to make new wood, leaves, twigs, fruits, and nuts. Some of a tree's food is used right away. Some is stored for future use.

Norway Maple

Almond

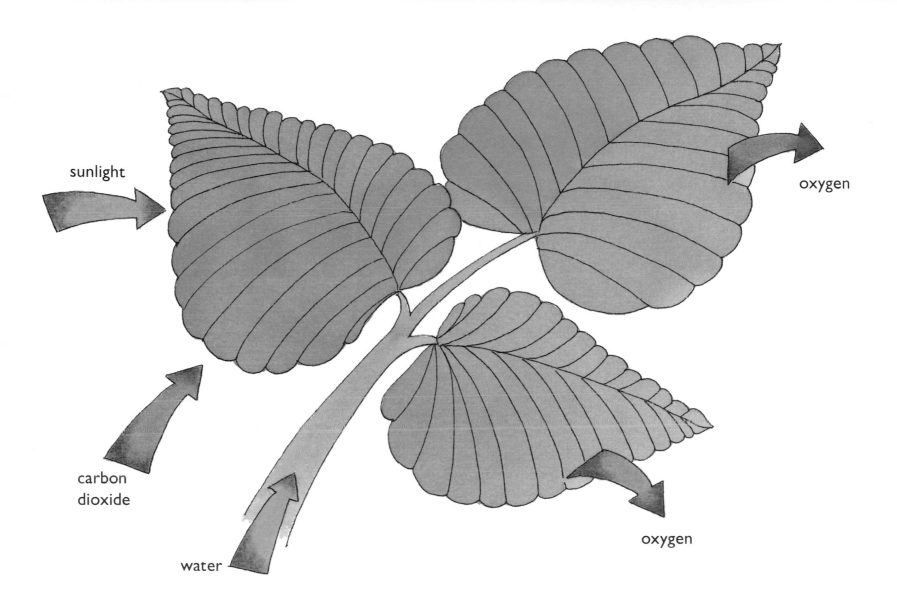

sunlight

oxygen

carbon
dioxide

oxygen

water

While making food, leaves also make oxygen that they
don't need. They get rid of it by putting it into the air.

Much of the oxygen that people and animals need comes from trees. Without them, we might not be here at all. So trees are more than nice—they're something we can't live without!

And that is why everyone should be a friend to trees.

How to Be a Friend to Trees

There are lots of things you can do to be a friend to trees. Here are a few. See how many more you can think of.

🌲 Using less paper is a great way to save trees.

If you can, use a rag, a sponge, or a dish towel instead of a paper towel.

🌲 Take along a paper bag when you go to market. Most bags can be used over again. No one needs new bags every time. Better yet, take your own net or canvas bag to market. Then you won't need the store's bags at all.

If you buy something small and don't need a bag, say "No, thanks."

🌲Do you usually write on only one side of a piece of paper? Don't throw it out. Use the other side for scrap paper.

🌲Recycling paper is another way to be a friend. When paper is recycled, it is shredded, mashed, washed, and made into paper again. Then we need less new paper. And that means fewer trees must be cut. Suppose all the people in the United States recycled their Sunday newspapers. That would save 500,000 trees a week! Does your family recycle? Do you help?

And then there is something else you can do, if you have the chance.

Help plant a tree.